This book belongs to . . .

Heart to Heart Publishing, Inc.

Heart to Heart Publishing, Inc.
528 Mud Creek Road • Morgantown, KY 42261
(270) 526-5589
www.hearttoheartpublishinginc.com

Copyright © 2015
Publishing Rights: Heart to Heart Publishing, Inc.
Publishing Date 2015
Library of Congress Control No. 2015944160
ISBN 978-1-937008-39-0

All rights reserved. No part of this book may be reproduced or utilized in any form or by any means, electronic or mechanical, including photocopying, recording, or by an information storage and retrieval system, without permission in writing. Fax to Permission Request (270) 526-7489.

Author: Terri Smith
Artist: Donna Brooks
Editor: L.J.Gill
Copy-Editor: Susan Mitchell
Designer: April Yingling-Jernigan
Photo credits : by Elizabeth Montgomery, subject- white Arabian "Catch" /
owner Leigh Montgomery

6-2-2015
54736-0
Printed in South Korea by Four Colour Print Group, Louisville, Kentucky,
first Publication 2015

First Edition
10 9 8 7 6 5 4 3 2

Heart to Heart Publishing, Inc. books are available at a special discount for bulk purchases in the US by corporations, institutions and other organizations. For more information, please contact Special Sales at 270-526-5589.

Dedication

In gratitude to God, who in all His goodness continues to humble with loving parents it is by that same love that I honor and dedicate my first book to Gus and Mabel Smith. May the love they planted continue to define my life works.

In gratitude for a sister, Karen Smith-Fruitman and brothers, Steven and Tim Smith may we continue to grow together and our tree continue to bear much fruit rooted in such love.

In gratitude for two sons and daughter-in-laws, James and Beth, Benjamin and Amy may you forever bloom in the goodness of family and Grandchildren, Collin, Morgan and Emma – thrive in the richness of such love.

Merry Christmas
Terri Smith

I dedicate this beautiful story to all the children that were not lucky enough to have parents like this Momma and Daddy. Each child has a right to have this sort of love. I hope each child will read this story and feel what true love feels like through this story. Know that God loves us all with this much love plus so much more.

~ Donna Brooks

My thanks........

Touched to have had such support in this heart felt endeavor, I am humbled and say thanks to so many for their encouragements. I have benefited greatly through this wonderful process and thank you for support in ways I am not aware of yet – as I know there have been angels masquerading as people along the way.

Thank you.

My thanks to Linda Hawkins of Heart to Heart Publishing Inc. for going above and beyond to bring my idea forward, Donna Brooks for her beautiful illustrations that captured the event and April Yingling-Jernigan, for binding together a labor of love! I am so grateful.

Thanks to the following: Donna Hirst, Leader of our Friday Group and prayer partners Sandy, Bets, Kay, Tina, and Leigh, and to Darra, Mary, Steph, and Lorrie for such encouragement. To Bob, Mary Lou, and Jordan, my thanks also as this would have not been possible with out such great love.

One White Christmas

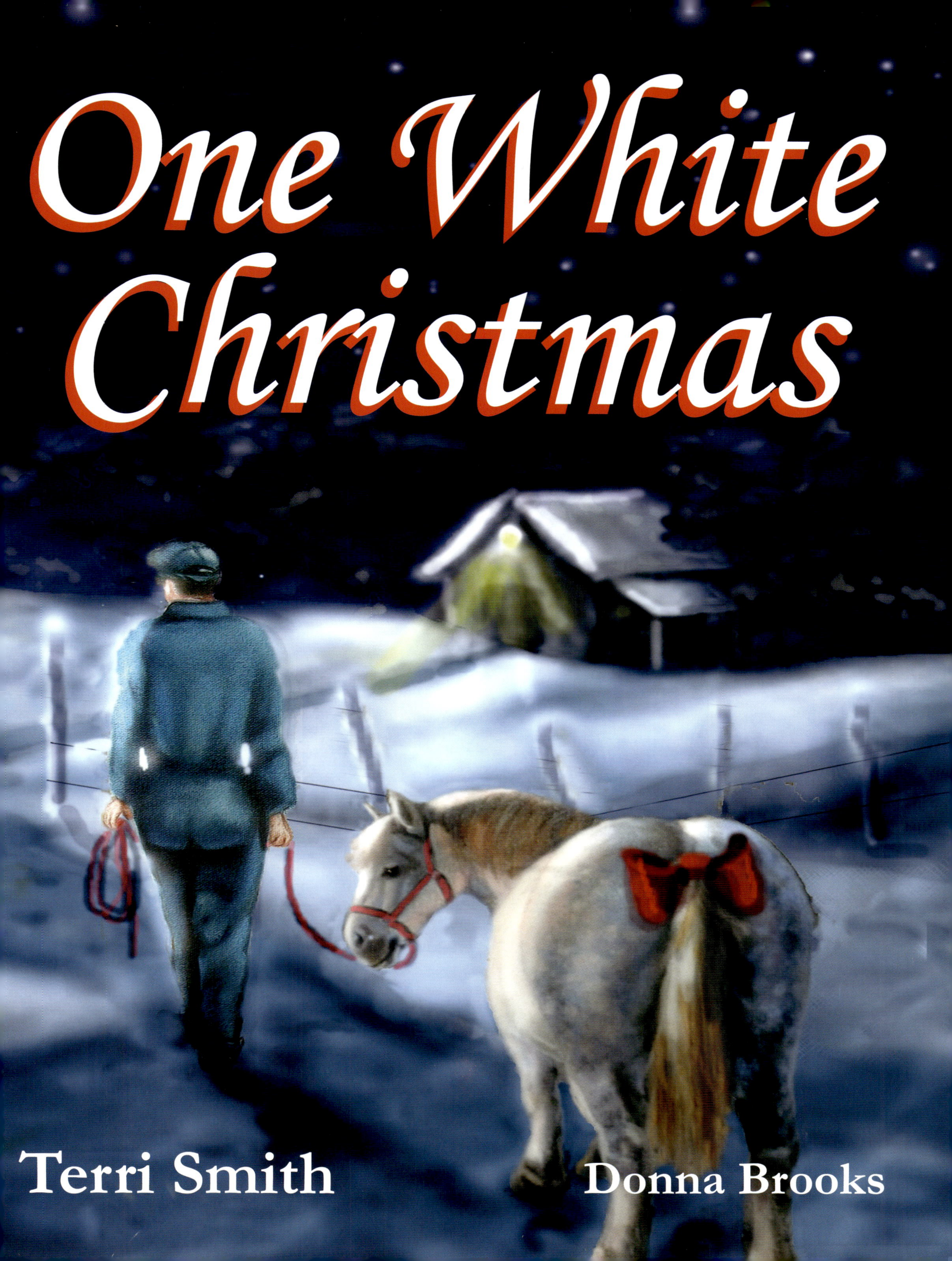

Terri Smith

Donna Brooks

And thick winter socks
Warmed little feet and small toes!

And we lay sniffing aromas
Of all mother prepared.

*Her floors were all polished
And Christmas ham baked*

The crackling fire warmed
Gathering around its soft glow

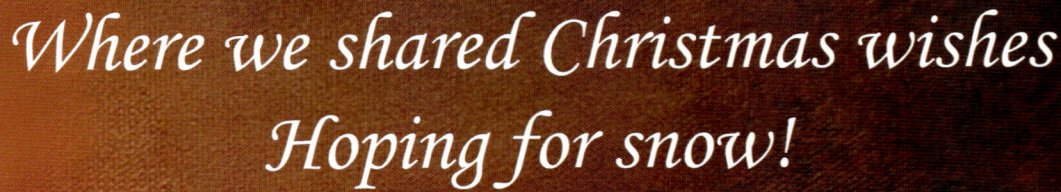

Where we shared Christmas wishes
Hoping for snow!

*Coal embers burned softly
Until pillows turned to clouds-*

Until some dreaming of snowballs
Dreamt them —out loud!

And we peeked out to listen
From four cozy bed sacks!

*The sound of hooves clopping
Clopped up our porch steps*

Then closing our eyes
Laying ever so still –

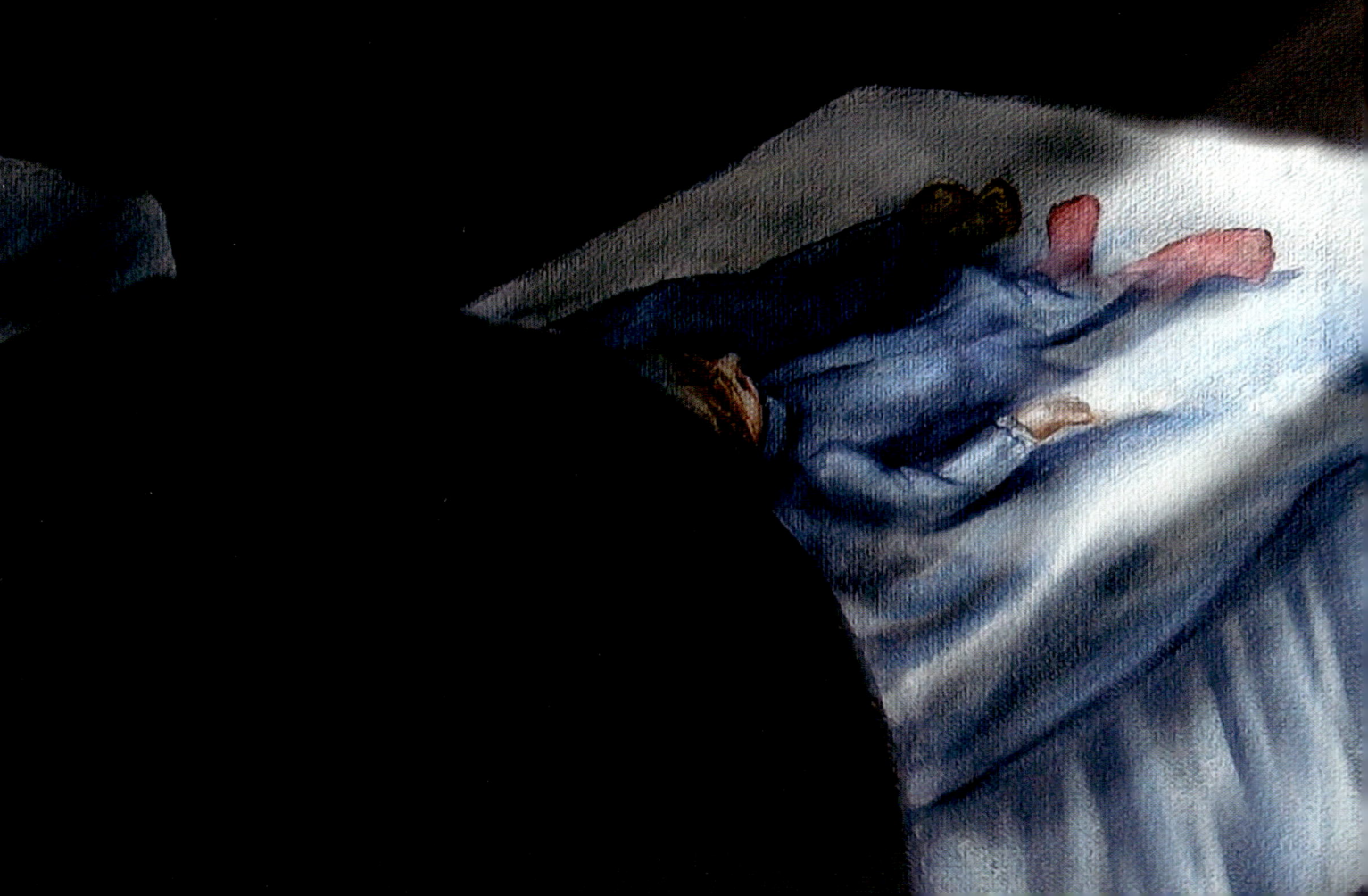

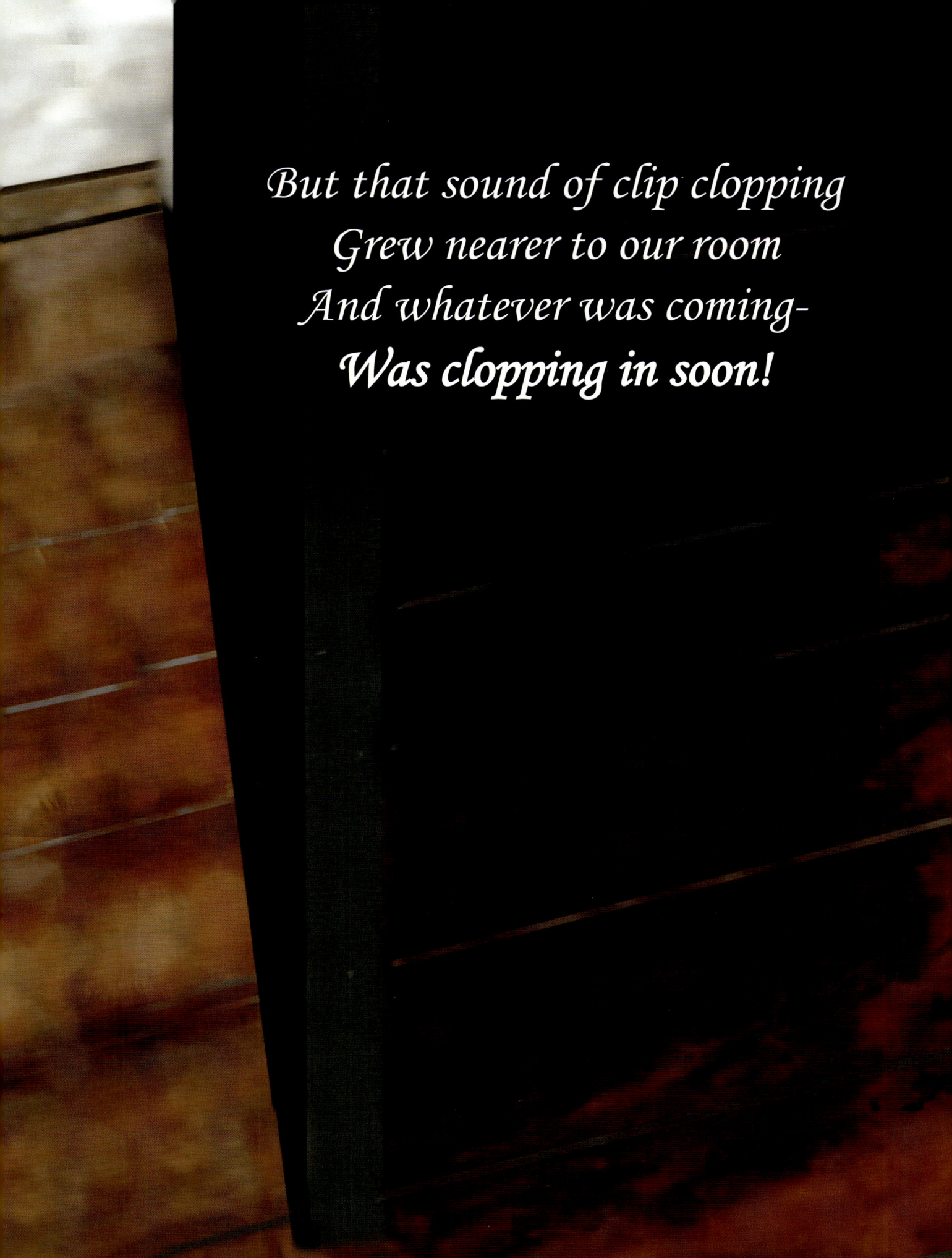

But that sound of clip clopping
Grew nearer to our room
And whatever was coming-
Was clopping in soon!

*Suddenly it grew quiet
And hearing nothing at all
One eye peeked open
Then spied a shaggy Snowball!*

*His snow white coat sparkled
But what sparkled more bright*

*Was the love in Dad's eyes
When he led us that night!*

We each took a turn
Through our home as he led
And as each one dismounted
Mother tucked into bed.

Down porch steps hooves followed
Making tracks in the snow
Following Dad to the barn
With his fancy red bow.

Love covered like a blanket
Of fresh fallen snow
And warmed like the light
Of a candle's soft glow.

We slumbered in awe!
Our hearts lay in delight!
We were warmed by the gift
Love had given that night!

Merry Christmas!

Hidden Hearts

Page 1 - Left lower window pane
Page 2 - Middle of tree to right of star
Page 3 - In glow on lamp shade
Page 5 - Door knob
Page 6 - On girl's wrist
Page 7 - In middle of door
Page 8 - On icing on cake
Page 9 - In glowing fire
Page 11 - In glow in snow ball
Page 12 - Beside 4th star
Page 13 - Dog collar
Page 14 - Top right corner
Page 15 - Horse hoof
Page 16 - Dog collar
Page 17 - Mom's robe
Page 18 - Dad's hat
Page 19 - Glow on foot of bed
Page 20 - Pony's bangs forelock
Page 21 - Right ankle
Page 25 - In glow on pony's shoulder
Page 26 - Above pocket on Dad's shirt
Page 27 - Glow on pony's hip
Page 28 - In glow of flame
Page 29 - On cross in window
Page 30 - In flow on hip
Page 31 - On pony's nose